A New Hospital Prayer Book

All booklets are published thanks to the generous support of the members of the Catholic Truth Society

Contents

Well loved prayers

"Listen with faith to His voice repeating to each of you 'Come to me all you labour and are overburdened and I will give you rest.'" – Pope John Paul II[1]

Our Father

Our Father, who art in heaven, hallowed be thy name. Thy kingdom come. Thy will be done on earth as it is in heaven. Give us this day our daily bread, and forgive us our trespasses, as we forgive those who trespass against us. And lead us not into temptation, but deliver us from evil. Amen.

Hail Mary

Hail Mary, full of grace, the Lord is with thee: blessed art thou among women and blessed is the fruit of thy womb, Jesus. Holy Mary, Mother of God, pray for us sinners, now, and at the hour of our death. Amen.

Glory be

Glory be to the Father, and to the Son, and to the Holy Spirit. As it was in the beginning, is now, and ever shall be, world without end. Amen.

Come Holy Spirit

Come, O Holy Spirit, fill the hearts of your faithful, and
enkindle in them the fire of your love.

V. Send forth your Spirit and they shall be created.

R. And you shall renew the face of the earth.

Let us pray. O God, who taught the hearts of the faithful
by the light of the Holy Spirit, grant that by the gift of the
same Spirit we may be always truly wise and ever rejoice
in his consolation. Through Christ, Our Lord. **R.** Amen.

Blessing

I thank you, Lord, for the wonder of my being, for giving
me another day to love and serve you. May I often think
of you during it!

Bless all Christian families, particularly my own loved
ones. May the light of your presence shine out to the
world from them. Lord, hear my prayer.

Comfort all who are patients in this hospital. Bring
them healing through the dedicated skill of the doctors
and nurses. Bless the many others who work behind the
scenes to support them. Lord, hear my prayer.

St Teresa of Avila's bookmark

Let nothing disturb you, let nothing affright you. All
things are passing. God never changes. Patient endurance
attains to all things. Who God possesses, in nothing is
wanting. Alone God suffices.

Prayer of St Francis

Lord, make me an instrument of Your peace, Where there is hatred, let me sow love, Where there is injury, pardon, Where there is doubt, faith, Where there is despair, hope, Where there is darkness, light, And where there is sadness, joy. O Divine Master, grant that I may not so much seek to be consoled, as to console, To be understood, as to understand, To be loved, as to love. For it is in giving that we receive, It is in pardoning, that we are pardoned, And it is in dying, that we are born to eternal life. Amen.

Act of Faith

My God, I believe in you, I trust in You, I love You above all things, with all my heart and mind and strength. I love You because You are supremely good and worth loving; and because I love You, I am sorry with all my heart for offending you. Lord, have mercy on me, a sinner. Amen.

Anima Christi

Soul of Christ, sanctify me. Body of Christ, heal me. Blood of Christ, drench me. Water from the side of Christ, wash me. Passion of Christ, strengthen me. Good Jesus, hear me. In Your wounds shelter me. From turning away keep me. From the evil one protect me. At the hour of my death call me. Into Your presence lead me, to praise You with all your saints for ever and ever. Amen.

Prayer of Charles de Foucauld

Father, I abandon myself into your hands; do with me what you will. Whatever you may do, I thank you: I am ready for all, I accept all. Let only your will be done in me, and in all your creatures. I wish no more than this, O Lord. Into your hands I commend my soul; I offer it to you with all the love of my heart, for I love you, Lord, and so need to give myself, to surrender myself into your hands, without reserve, and with boundless confidence, for you are my Father.

Your will be done

In all things may the most holy, the most just, and the most lovable will of God be done, praised, and exalted above all forever. Your will be done, O Lord, Your will be done. The Lord has given, the Lord has taken away; blessed be the name of the Lord.

Act of Trust

Lord, your will be done. I offer up to you my sufferings, together with all that my Saviour has suffered for me; and I beg of you, through His sufferings, to have mercy on me. Free me from this illness and pain if you will, and if it be for my good. You love me too much to let me suffer unless it be for my good. Therefore O Lord, I trust myself to you; do with me as you please. In sickness and in health, I wish to love you always.

Cardinal Newman's prayer

O Lord, support us all the day long until the shadows lengthen and evening comes, and the busy world is hushed, and the fever of life is over, and our work is done. Then, in your mercy, grant us a safe lodging, and a holy rest, and peace at last.

Prayer to Christ the healer

In the comfort of your love, I pour out to you, my Saviour the memories that haunt me, the anxieties that perplex me, the fears that stifle me, the sickness that prevails upon me, and the frustration of all the pain that weaves about within me. Lord, help me to see your peace in my turmoil, your compassion in my sorrow, your forgiveness in my weakness, and your love in my need. Touch me, O Lord, with your healing power and strength.

The Lord is my shepherd

The Lord is my shepherd, I lack nothing.
In meadows of green grass he lets me lie.
To the waters of repose he leads me;
there he revives my soul.
He guides me by paths of virtue
for the sake of his name.
Though I pass through a gloomy valley,
I fear no harm;

beside me your rod and your staff are there,
to hearten me.
You prepare a table before me
under the eyes of my enemies;
you anoint my head with oil, my cup brims over.
Ah, how goodness and kindness pursue me,
every day of my life;
my home, the house of the Lord as long as I live!
(*Ps* 23:1-6)

Prayer of St Ignatius of Loyola

Take Lord and receive all my liberty, my memory, my understanding and my will; all that I have and possess you have given to me; and to you I give it all back. It is all yours; Dispose of it according to your Will. Give me only your love and your grace; this alone suffices for me.

The Lord is with you

Be still and be comforted; the Lord is with you,
strengthening and supporting you.
Put your trust in him for he loves and cares for you.
Listen to Jesus when he says, "Peace be still"
and believe that he is with you, and will help you always.
(*Harold Winstone*)

A prayer for inner peace

Take some time to be quiet in yourself, closing your eyes, and simply pause to breath in and out, experiencing peace for a few moments, and then breathe in and out repeating several times the words:

Jesus in your love,
Have mercy on me

Prayer before a Crucifix

Behold, O kind and most sweet Jesus, I cast myself on my knees in your sight, and with the most fervent desire of my soul, I pray and beseech you that you would impress upon my heart lively sentiments of faith, hope, and charity, with a true repentance for my sins, and a firm desire of amendment, while with deep affection and grief of soul I ponder within myself and mentally contemplate your five most precious wounds; having before my eyes that which David spoke in prophecy of you, O good Jesus: 'They pierced my hands and my feet; they have numbered all my bones'.

Some Hospital Prayers

"You that bear the weight of suffering occupy the first place among those whom God loves. As with those he met along the roads of Palestine, Jesus directs a gaze full of tenderness at you, His love will never be lacking."
– Pope John Paul II[2]

Let your God love you

Be silent, Be still. Alone. Empty. Before your God. Say nothing. Ask nothing. Be silent. Let your God look upon you. That is all. He knows. He understands. He loves you with an enormous love. He only wants to look upon you with his love. Quiet. Still be. Let your God - love you.
(*Ewina Gately, Psalms of a Laywoman*)

Going into hospital

Lord, help me, I am dreading going into hospital. There will be no privacy, but people continually about, bustling and noisy. I will never have any peace and quiet in which to pray to you. For even in the night people call out, nurses rush around and talk loudly. Lord, give me a sense of your presence deep within me, and a sense of peace that will persist under all the fuss and bother, for I need your help if I am to remain unflustered and serene.

Before the doctor's visit

O God, I can no longer pretend to myself that everything will be all right if I just leave things alone. I can no longer avoid the fact that there is something wrong. Go with me when I see my doctor today, and give me courage to face the truth about myself. Make me quite sure that whatever the verdict, I can face it with you. Let me remember the promise of God: When you pass through the waters I will be with you. (*William Barclay*)

Accepting sickness

Do not look forward to what might happen tomorrow; the same Everlasting Father who cares for you today, will take care of you tomorrow and every day. Either he will shield you from suffering or he will give you unfailing strength to bear it. Be at peace, then, and put aside all anxious thoughts and imaginings. (*St Francis de Sales*)

Before an operation

Jesus, I am very afraid. I do not know what is going to happen to me. I have absolutely no control over what happens and I dislike not being in control. I am afraid of the loss of consciousness that the anaesthetic will bring. I worry that I will be a burden to others after the operation and that I will not be so active again. Lord, help me to trust you. Arrange my life even though it may mean 'my being taken where I would rather not go'. (*John* 21) Let me realise if I die now I will be coming to you whose love casts out fear.

Prayer of waiting

God our Father, your Son Jesus Christ has entered into our broken world to heal our hearts and guide our lives. He shared in our human loneliness: the loneliness of the unfamiliar, the loneliness of the desert, the loneliness of waiting. I too am waiting and it seems so hard to take. As time goes by, I am getting more nervous and impatient. All the unknown makes my waiting an agony in itself. As I am lying here the hours seem like days and days like a lifetime. I never knew that waiting could be so painful! It feels like I am left hanging in the middle of nowhere without knowing exactly where I am going or what I am dealing with.

And I find myself looking through the door waiting for the doctor or the nurse to appear and at the same time fearing what they may say, or I catch myself looking through the window waiting for the day because the night has been too long for me.

O Lord, set my heart free from restlessness and let me trust in you. Amen.

God's loving plan

Since I too have shared the experience of illness several times in recent years, I have come to understand more and more clearly its value for my Petrine ministry and for the Church's life itself.

In expressing my affectionate solidarity to those who are suffering, I invite them to contemplate with faith the mystery of Christ crucified and risen, in order to discover God's loving plan in their own experience of pain.

Only by looking at Jesus, 'a man of sorrows, and acquainted with grief (*Isaiah* 53:3)' is it possible to find serenity and trust. – *Pope John Paul II*[3]

Prayer before surgery

O Lord, the hours seem so long as they go by. I am so restless and there are so many thoughts going through my mind, thoughts about the outcome of my surgery, about my future, about my family. I have fear and anxiety because it is my own body, my own life that's at stake. I raise my voice to you, O Lord, so that you may replace my fears with trust, my anxiety with faith in your healing human instruments. Bless the doctors who will operate on me. Guide their hands to bring healing where there is sickness, strength where there is weakness. Bless my family who, through their presence and support, have given me so much strength to face this moment. Bless my night. Make me rest peacefully under your protection so that I'll be ready for my important day tomorrow. Amen.

Help me to keep on

Lord, I can't pray much; I am too busy just enduring, just keeping on. You know I want to pray and that my whole being wants to be open to you though I can't do much about it actively. Accept my intention to love you and never let your Spirit cease to pray in the depth of my being.

Prayer in time of pain

O Lord, my Shepherd. I don't remember any more the pain of yesterday. I don't know about the pain of tomorrow. But, please, help me handle and accept the pain of today.

Give me the human and spiritual strength I need to bear it. Help me remember your cross, your prayer to the Father, your attitude. Free me from the tendency to feel sorry for myself, from my need to complain about things and people around me. I just don't appreciate long visits any more, or the efforts of friends to cheer me up.

Guide me to see your love made present in the faces of the people who care for me. Help me discover in the voices that break the silence of my day the comfort and promise of a life renewed. Amen.

Pain

I am overwhelmed by pain, and my failure to bear it well; my heart is cold and my mind distracted. I offer all my suffering and failure to you to be united with your Son's cross and passion. I am nothing and have nothing except the pain; do what you want with it and me.

In pain and physical distress

Lord Jesus, you know what pain is like. You know the torture of the scourge upon your back, the sting of the thorns upon your brow, the agony of the nails in your hands. You know what I'm going through just now. Help me to bear my pain gallantly, cheerfully and patiently, and help me to remember that I will never be tried above what I am able to bear, and that you are with me. (*William Barclay*)

Use of pain

We ask you not, O Lord, to rid us of pain; but grant us in your mercy that our pain may be free from waste, unfretted by rebellion against your will, unsoiled by thought of ourselves, purified by love of our kind and ennobled by devotion to your Kingdom, through the merits of your only Son, our Lord. (*Henry S. Nash*)

Suffering courageously

O God, who exalted the Crucified, the Son, by a triumphant resurrection and ascension into heaven: may his triumphs and glories so shine in the eyes of our hearts and minds, that we may more clearly comprehend his sufferings, and more courageously pass through our own. (*Eric Milner-White*)

In a long hospitalisation

O Lord, it has been a while since I've walked on grass or seen the stars in the sky. So many silent and restless nights, so many long and boring days on a hospital bed. At first I was too sick to care, but now I am getting impatient to go home. I get upset about my dependency, my setbacks, my slow progress. But since, O Lord, you have taken me this far, since you have given me enough patience to endure each day, I pray again that you may bring healing to that which still needs to be healed in me. Let my hope and motivation overcome the times of discouragement and impatience so that I may soon breathe fresh air and enjoy the atmosphere of my own home.

Prayer for my family

O Lord, I thank you for the gift of my family, for the love, strength and comfort they have given me during my illness.

Watch over them and protect them every day, particularly now that I am away from them. Help them to adjust to my absence by coming closer together, by becoming sensitive to each other's needs and by setting aside their differences.

Make this a special moment in our lives when we discover more deeply our love for each other, our need for our common faith in you.

Prayer of thanksgiving

O Lord, I thank you for touching my life during this time of sickness, for widening my horizon and deepening my understanding of your truth.

You have opened my eyes so that I could see the signs of your presence. You provided me with time to reflect upon myself, my past, my values, my problems and my life.

Somehow a lot of things that until yesterday seemed to be important, are insignificant today and I have learned to really appreciate the simple blessings of every day. It seems as if I woke up from a hazy dream. For all of this, I thank you. Amen.

Stations of the Cross

"Do not be afraid of death. Welcome it when it comes. It is now a holy thing, made so by him who died that we might live." - Cardinal Basil Hume OSB[4]

How to meditate each station of the Cross

Consider the Station, then say

V. *We adore you, O Christ, and praise you.*
R. *Because by your holy Cross you have redeemed the world.*

Then consider the Reflection and say the Prayer, followed by:

I love you, Jesus, my love, above all things; I repent with my whole heart of having offended you. Never permit me to separate myself from you again. Grant that I may love you always; and then do with me what you will.
Our Father, Hail Mary, Glory be.

Opening Prayer

O Jesus Christ, my Lord, with what great love did you pass over the painful road which led you to death; and I, how often have I abandoned you! But now I love you with my whole soul, and because I love you I am sincerely sorry for having offended you. My Jesus, pardon me and permit me to accompany you in this journey. You are going to die for love of me, and it is my wish also, my dearest Redeemer, to die for love of you. My Jesus, in your love I wish to live. In your love I wish to die.

1. Jesus is condemned to death

Reflection: Consider how Jesus, after having been scourged and crowned with thorns, was unjustly condemned by Pilate to die on the Cross.

Prayer: My loving Jesus, it was not Pilate; no, it was my sins that condemned you to die. I beseech you, by the merits of this sorrowful journey, to assist my soul in her journey towards eternity. *I love you, Jesus...*

At the Cross her station keeping,
Stood the mournful mother weeping,
Close to Jesus to the last.

2. Jesus receives the Cross

Reflection: Consider how Jesus, in making this journey with the Cross on his shoulders, thought of us, and offered for us to his Father the death he was about to undergo.

Prayer: My most beloved Jesus! I embrace all the tribulations you have destined for me until death. I beseech you, by the merits of the pain you suffered in carrying your Cross, to give me the necessary help to carry mine with perfect patience and resignation. *I love...*

Through her heart his sorrow sharing,
All his bitter anguish bearing,
Now at length the sword has passed.

3. Jesus falls the first time

Reflection: Consider this first fall of Jesus under his Cross. His flesh was torn by the scourges, his head was crowned with thorns; he had lost a great quantity of blood. So weakened he could scarcely walk, he yet had to carry this great load upon his shoulders. The soldiers struck him rudely and he fell several times.

Prayer: My Jesus, it is the weight, not of the Cross, but of my sins, which has made you suffer so much pain. By the merits of this first fall, deliver me from the misfortune of falling into mortal sin. *I love...*

Oh, how sad and sore distressed
Was that mother highly blessed
Of the sole-begotten one!

4. Jesus is met by his blessed mother

Reflection: Consider the meeting of the Son and the mother, which took place on this journey. Their looks became like so many arrows to wound those hearts which love each other so tenderly.

Prayer: My sweet Jesus, by the sorrow you experienced in this meeting, grant me the grace of a devoted love for your holy mother. And you, my queen, who were overwhelmed with sorrow, obtain for me a continual and tender remembrance of the passion of your Son. *I love...*

Christ above in torments hangs;
She beneath beholds the pangs
Of her dying glorious Son.

5. The Cross is laid upon Simon of Cyrene

Reflection: Consider how his cruel tormentors, seeing Jesus was on the point of expiring, and fearing he would die on the way, whereas they wished him to die the shameful death of the Cross, constrained Simon of Cyrene to carry the Cross behind our Lord.

Prayer: My most beloved Jesus, by your grace I will not refuse to carry the Cross; I accept it, I embrace it. I accept in particular the death you have destined for me, with all the pains which may accompany it; I unite it to your death, I offer it to You. You have died for love of me; I will die for love of you. Help me by your grace. *I love...*

Is there one who would not weep,
Whelmed in miseries so deep,
Christ's dear mother to behold?

6. Veronica wipes the face of Jesus

Reflection: Consider how the holy woman named Veronica, seeing Jesus so ill-used, and bathed in sweat and blood, wiped his face with a towel, on which was left the impression of his holy countenance.

Prayer: My most beloved Jesus! Your face was beautiful before, but in this journey it has lost all its beauty, and wounds and blood have disfigured it. Alas! My soul also was once beautiful, when it received your grace in baptism; but I have disfigured it by my sins; you alone, my Redeemer, can restore it to its former beauty. Do this by your passion, O Jesus! *I love...*

Can the human heart refrain,
From partaking in her pain,
In that mother's pain untold?

7. Jesus falls the second time

Reflection: Consider the second fall of Jesus under the Cross; a fall which renews the pain of all the wounds in his head and members.

Prayer: My Jesus, how many times have you pardoned me, and how many times have I fallen again, and begun again to offend you. By the merits of this second fall, give me the help necessary to persevere in your grace until death. Grant that in all temptations which assail me I may always commend myself to you. *I love...*

Bruised, derided, cursed, defiled,
She beheld her tender Child,
All with bloody scourges rent.

8. The women of Jerusalem mourn for our Lord

Reflection: Consider how these women wept with compassion at seeing Jesus in such a pitiable state, streaming with blood as he walked along. 'Daughters of Jerusalem', he said, 'weep not for me, but for yourselves and for your children'.

Prayer: My Jesus, laden with sorrows! I weep for the offences I have committed against you because of the pains they have deserved, and still more because of the displeasure they have caused you, who have loved me so much. It is your love more than the fear of hell, which causes me to weep for my sins. *I love...*

For the sins of his own nation,
Saw him hang in desolation,
Till his spirit forth he sent.

9. Jesus falls the third time

Reflection: Consider the third fall of Jesus Christ. His weakness was extreme, and the cruelty of his executioners excessive, who tried to hasten his steps when he could scarcely move.

Prayer: My outraged Jesus, by the merits of the weakness You suffered in going to Calvary, give me strength to conquer all human respect, and my wicked passions, which have led me to despise your friendship. *I love...*

O thou mother! fount of love!
Touch my spirit from above.
Make my heart with yours accord.

10. Jesus is stripped of his garments

Reflection: Consider the violence with which Jesus was stripped by the executioners. His inner garments adhered to his torn flesh, and they dragged them off so roughly that the skin came with them. Compassionate your Saviour thus cruelly treated.

Prayer: My most innocent Jesus! by the merits of the torment you have felt, help me to strip myself of all affection to things of earth, that I may place all my love in you, who are so worthy of my love. *I love...*

Make me feel as you have felt;
Make my soul to glow and melt,
With the love of Christ my Lord.

11. Jesus is nailed to the Cross

Reflection: Consider how Jesus, having been placed upon the Cross, extended his hands, and offered to his eternal Father the sacrifice of his life for our salvation. Those barbarians fastened him with nails, and then, securing the Cross, allowed him to die with anguish on this infamous gibbet.

Prayer: My Jesus, loaded with contempt, nail my heart to your feet, that it may ever remain there, to love you, and never more to leave you. *I love...*

Holy mother! pierce me through;
In my heart each wound renew,
Of my Saviour crucified.

12. Jesus dies on the Cross

Reflection: Consider how Jesus, being consumed with anguish after three hours' agony on the Cross, abandoned himself to the weight of his body, bowed his head and died.

Prayer: O my dying Jesus! I kiss devoutly the Cross on which you died for love of me. I have merited by my sins to die a miserable death, but your death is my hope. By the merits of your death, give me grace to die embracing your feet, and burning with love for you. I commit my soul into your hands. *I love...*

Let me share with you his pain,
Who for all my sins was slain,
Who for me in torments died.

13. Jesus is taken down from the Cross

Reflection: Consider how, after Our Lord had expired, two of his disciples, Joseph and Nicodemus, took him down from the Cross, and placed him in the arms of his afflicted Mother, who received him with unutterable tenderness, and pressed him to her bosom.

Prayer: O Mother of Sorrow, for the love of this Son, accept me for your servant, and pray for me. And you, my Redeemer, since you have died for me, permit me to love you; for I wish but you, and nothing more. *I love...*

Let me mingle tears with you,
Mourning him who mourned for me,
All the days that I may live.

14. Jesus is laid in the sepulchre

Reflection: Consider how the disciples, accompanied by his holy mother, carried the body of Jesus to bury it. They closed the tomb, and all came sorrowfully away.

Prayer: My buried Jesus! I kiss the stone that encloses you. But you rose again on the third day. I beseech you, by your resurrection, to make me rise in glory with you at the last day, to be always united with you in heaven, to praise you and love you for ever. *I love...*

By the Cross with you to stay;
There with you to weep and pray,
Is all I ask of you to give.

Prayers to Our Lady

*"Dear brothers and sisters who experience suffering in a
particular way... find your inspiration in Mary,
Mother of love and human pain." – Pope John Paul II*[5]

Hail Mary

Hail Mary, full of grace, the Lord is with thee: blessed art
thou among women and blessed is the fruit of thy womb,
Jesus. Holy Mary, Mother of God, pray for us sinners,
now, and at the hour of our death. Amen.

Prayer of John Paul II

I pray that Mary, Health of the Sick,
will continue to grant her loving protection
to all who are wounded in body or spirit,
and will intercede for those who care for them.
May she help us to unite our sufferings
with those of her Son,
as we journey in joyful hope
to the safety of the Father's House.

Memorare

Remember, O most gracious Virgin Mary that never was it
known that anyone who fled to thy protection, implored thy

help or sought thy intercession, was left unaided. Inspired with this confidence, I fly unto thee, O Virgin of virgins, my mother; to thee do I come before thee I stand, sinful and sorrowful, O Mother of the Word Incarnate, despise not my petitions, but in thy mercy hear and answer me. Amen.

Hail Holy Queen

Hail, Holy Queen, Mother of Mercy. Hail, our life, our sweetness and our hope to thee do we cry poor banished children of Eve to thee do we send up our sighs mourning and weeping in this valley of tears. Turn then O most gracious advocate thine eyes of mercy towards us and after this our exile show unto us the blessed fruit of thy womb, Jesus. Amen.

Regina Coeli

Queen of Heaven rejoice, Alleluia
For He whom thou wast worthy to bear, Alleluia
Has risen as He said, Alleluia.
Pray for us to God, Alleluia.
Rejoice and be glad, O Virgin Mary, Alleluia
For the Lord has truly risen, Alleluia

Let us pray. O God, who didst deign to give joy to the world by the resurrection of your Son, Our Lord Jesus Christ Grant that through the intercession of the Virgin Mary, his Mother, we may enter into the joys of eternal life. Through Christ Our Lord. Amen.

We fly to you

We fly to your patronage,
O Holy Mother of God;
despise not our petitions in our needs,
but deliver us from all dangers,
O Glorious and blessed Virgin.

Prayer to Mary

Most Pure virgin, you are the health of the sick, the refuge of sinners, the consolation of the afflicted and the dispenser of all graces.

In my weakness and discouragement, I appeal today to the treasures of your divine mercy and goodness, and I dare to call you by the sweet name of Mother.

Yes, O Mother, attend me in my infirmity, give me bodily health, so that I may do my duties with vitality and joy, and with the same disposition may I serve your Son Jesus and give thanks to you, health of the sick. Our Lady of Good Health, pray for us.

THE HOLY ROSARY

The Rosary prayer begins with the *Sign of the Cross* (at the Crucifix) followed by reciting the *Apostles' Creed*.

On the round beads say the *Our Father*, and on the oval beads say the *Hail Mary*. After each series of Hail Mary's say the *Glory Be*.

During the prayers on each series of ten beads (decade), we meditate on one of the Mysteries of the Rosary as listed below. End the Rosary with the *Hail Holy Queen*.

The Joyful Mysteries

(Mondays and Saturdays)

1. The Annunciation (*Luke* 1:26-38)
2. The Visitation (*Luke* 1: 39-56)
3. The Nativity (*Luke* 2:1-20)
4. The Presentation (*Luke* 2:21-38)
5. The Finding of Jesus in the Temple (*Luke* 2:41-52)

The Luminous Mysteries

(Thursdays)

1. Jesus' Baptism in the Jordan (2 *Corinthians* 5:21, *Matthew* 3:17 and parallels)
2. Jesus' self-manifestation at the wedding of Cana (*John* 2:1- 12
3. Jesus' proclamation of the Kingdom of God, with His call to conversion (*Mark* 1:15, *Mark* 2:3-13; *Luke* 7:47- 48, *John* 20:22-23)
4. Jesus' Transfiguration (*Luke* 9:35 and parallels)
5. Jesus' institution of the Eucharist, as the sacramental expression of the Paschal Mystery. (*Luke* 24:13-35 and parallels, 1 *Corinthians* 11:24-25)

The Sorrowful Mysteries

(Tuesdays and Fridays)

1. The Agony in the Garden (*Matthew* 26:36-46, *Luke* 22:39-46)

2. The Scourging at the Pillar (*Matthew* 27:26, *Mark* 15:15, *John* 19:1)

3. The Crowning with Thorns (*Matthew* 27:27-30, Mark 15:16-20, *John* 19:2)

4. The Carrying of the Cross (*Matthew* 27:31-32, *Mark* 15:21, *Luke* 23:26-32, *John* 19:17)

5. The Crucifixion (*Matthew* 27:33-56, *Mark* 15:22-39, *Luke* 23:33-49, *John* 19:17-37)

The Glorious Mysteries

(Wednesdays and Sundays)

1. The Resurrection (*Matthew* 28:1-8, *Mark* 16:1-18, *Luke* 24:1-12, *John* 20:1-29)

2. The Ascension (*Mark* 16:19-20, *Luke* 24:50-53, *Acts* 1:6-11)

3. The Descent of the Holy Ghost (*Acts* 2:1-13)

4. The Assumption of Our Blessed Lady. (*Rev* 12:1)

5. The Coronation of Our Lady Blessed as Queen of Heaven. (*Rev* 12:1)

Prayers for Expectant Mothers

"How important it is always to have in the back of our minds, to be able to bring to the front in times of need, the great conviction of God's special care and interest in each one of us." - Cardinal Basil Hume OSB

Prayer for a child in the womb

Almighty God, author of life, I thank you for the gift of new life. Bless our child in my womb. Protect him or her from all harm. Grant that he or she will be a healthy child. Grant that he or she will receive the Sacrament of Baptism and grow up in grace to serve you and the Church. I make my prayer through Christ our Lord. Amen.

Prayer for a safe delivery

Lord, the months of waiting are ended and my time is almost here. Take away all tension and fear; make me relaxed and unafraid. Strengthen me for my delivery and give me joy in remembering that through me you are sending another human person into the world. Amen.

Thanksgiving after delivery

Lord, thank you for bringing me and my baby safely through everything. Bless my baby. Keep him/her safe in all the dangers of childhood. Bring him/her safely through the hazards of youth and grant that he/she may grow up to be a fully mature person.

Help me always to be a good mother to the baby you have now given to me; to be kind, loving and understanding. Help me to teach him/her to love God and love his/her neighbour as Jesus himself came on earth to teach us. Bless me now. Amen.

Dedication of a child to Mary

Mary, Mother of God, take this child under your tender care. Watch over him/her always. Grant that his/her journey through this world may lead to eternal life. We ask this through Christ our Lord. Amen.

Prayer for a newborn baby

O Lord, you are the giver of all life, human and divine. You came into the world so that we might have life in fullness.

We are grateful for the life you have given us and for making us bearers of life to other people.

We rejoice for the miracle of the new life that has been born into our midst, for choosing us as instruments of this new creation.

As you have given us the joy of being life-givers, help us to share our love and care with this baby who is already part of our family.

Send your blessing upon our child to protect him/her and your Holy Spirit upon him to guide him/her throughout his life. Amen.

Prayer of parents

Heavenly Father, you have given to us the opportunity and responsibility of bringing new life into the world. Bless us in our joys and sorrows. Deepen our love for one another and for our children. We are the first bearers of your word and your love to them. Remind us often that we have no riches or training to give them without you. Amen.

Prayer for a sick baby

Lord, I pray to you for my baby who is sick. If it is your will, grant that he/she may be brought to perfect health. Amen.

Prayer on the death of a child

When our child's absence is all we feel,
God be near us.
When our bodies ache to hold our child,
God be near us.
When the world goes on as if nothing's happened,
God be near us.

When our lives are dark, desolate, cold,
Hold us Lord.
When we long to be dead to stop the pain,
Hold us Lord.
When we scream our 'whys?' at you,
Hold us Lord.

Jesus, you cried at the death of your friend,
You share in our sorrow.
Jesus, you shouted from the Cross,
   'Why have you forsaken me?'
You share in our fear.
Jesus, in death's agony and the tomb's emptiness,
You share in our loneliness.

You who feel our despair and depression,
Give us faith.
You who understand the times we want to hide,
Give us hope.
You who know when our hearts are broken,
Give us love.

Be near us and hold us, safe in your promise,
We shall be together again. Amen.

Scripture Readings and Ways to Pray

"Saint Augustine wrote 'What will you worry about? What will you be anxious for? He who made you will take care of you. Will he who took care of you before you came into being not take care of you now?'"
–Pope John Paul II[6]

Many say, 'I just can't pray'. I just do not have it in me to pray to God. Hospital is not the place. I am too worried, too busy with my thoughts. There is no privacy. I do not have the energy to read. I am in too much pain. I cannot concentrate on a prayer book. My spirit is arid. If not, then my flesh is too weak.

One way to pray is to be where you are and call quietly to the Lord from your heart. Do so only as you can, not as you think you should.

Sit or lie as relaxed as you can. If possible, close your eyes. Listening to the sounds that surround you, identify them and then let them fade. Enter deeply into yourself from your mind - 'the crazy woman of the house' as St Teresa of Avila says - and into your heart. This can be a gentle struggle. Do not give in to distractions, or itches, or restlessness. Be patient. Persevere.

Let a cry come from your heart to your beloved. Cry out to him slowly, purposefully from your spirit. Repeat your cry again and again. Ask him and speak to him. Remember always that God loves you, that God knows you, your hopes, your sufferings.

Continue in this way for as long as you can; five minutes, ten minutes, until you want to stop. Then say the Our Father slowly, and ask God to be with you, and to help you to be and accept where you are, now.

You might want to do this every day. You may need to do it whenever fear or anguish or worries come to you. Remember that Christ is always there. He runs to the humble, to the weak. From the haughty he keeps afar.

As you pray in this way you may pray with one phrase, slowly over and over on your lips until it takes hold of your heart:

Lord help me!
Support and strengthen me Lord!
Lord, help me to keep going.
My Lord and my God.
Lord you are my strength and help.
My trust is in you, O Lord, you are my God.
Lord, give me back my sight.
Lord, heal me.
Out of the depths I cry to you O Lord,
Lord hear my prayer.
Jesus of Nazareth have mercy on me a sinner.

SCRIPTURE PASSAGES

You may want to read, or have read to you, one of the short scripture passages which follow. Meditate on them. How do they strike you? What is the Lord saying to you? Take a phrase from it and keep it in your heart and repeat it over and over. The Lord is slow to anger, rich in mercy. He loves you and will help you.

Though I walk in the shadow of death, I will fear no evil for you are with me (*Psalm* 22:4).

Come blessed of my Father, says the Lord Jesus, and take possession of the kingdom prepared for you (*Matthew* 25:24).

Truly I say to you: Today you will be with me in paradise, says the Lord Jesus (*Luke* 23:43).

There are many rooms in my Father's house; if there were not, I should have told you (*John* 14:2).

I am going now to prepare a place for you, and after I have gone and prepared you a place, I shall return to take you with me (*John* 14:2-3).

Matthew 8:5-10, 13-17

When he went into Capernaum a centurion came up and pleaded with him, 'Sir', he said 'my servant is lying at home paralysed, and in great pain'. 'I will come myself and cure him' said Jesus. The centurion replied, 'Sir, I am not worthy to have you under my roof; just give the word and my servant will be cured. For I am under authority myself, and have soldiers under me; and I say to one man: Go, and he goes; to another: Come here, and he comes; to my servant: Do this, and he does it'. When Jesus heard this he was astonished and said to those following him, 'I tell you solemnly, nowhere in Israel have I found faith like this...' And to the centurion Jesus said, 'Go back, then; you have believed, so let this be done for you'. And the servant was cured at that moment. And going into Peter's house Jesus found Peter's mother-in-law in bed with fever. He touched her hand and the fever left her, and she got up and began to wait on him. That evening they brought him many who were possessed by devils. He cast out the spirits with a word and cured all who were sick. This was to fulfil the prophecy of Isaiah: He took our sicknesses away and carried our diseases for us.

Mark 2:1-12

When Jesus returned to Capernaum some time later, word went round that he was back; and so many people collected that there was no room left, even in front of he door. He

was preaching the word to them when some people came
bringing him a paralytic carried by four men, but as the
crowd made it impossible to get the man to him, they
stripped the roof over the place where Jesus was; and when
they had made an opening, they lowered the stretcher on
which the paralytic lay. Seeing their faith, Jesus said to the
paralytic, 'My child, your sins are forgiven'. Now some
scribes were sitting there, and they thought to themselves.
'How can this man talk like that? He is blaspheming. Who
can forgive sins but God.' Jesus, inwardly aware that this
was what they were thinking, said to them, 'Why do you
have these thoughts in your hearts? Which of these is
easier: to say to the paralytic, 'Your sins are forgiven' or to
say, 'Get up, pick up your stretcher and walk'? But to
prove to you that the Son of Man has authority on earth to
forgive sins' - he said to the paralytic - 'I order you: get up,
pick up your stretcher, and go off home'. And the man got
up, picked up his stretcher at once and walked out in front
of everyone, so that they were all astounded and praised
God saying, 'We have never seen anything like this'.

John 6:54-58

'Anyone who does eat my flesh and drink my blood has
eternal life, and I shall raise him up on the last day. For
my flesh is real food and my blood is real drink. He who
eats my flesh and drinks my blood lives in me and I live
in him. As I, who am sent by the living Father, myself

draw life from the Father, so whoever eats me will draw life from me. This is the bread come down from heaven; not like the bread our ancestor ate: they are dead, but anyone who eats this bread will live forever'.

Matthew 11:25-30

At that time, Jesus exclaimed, 'I bless you, Father, Lord of heaven and of earth, for hiding these things from the learned and the clever and revealing them to mere children. Yes, Father, for that is what it pleased you to do. Everything has been entrusted to me by my Father; and no one knows the Son except the Father, just as no one knows the Father except the Son and those to whom the Son chooses to reveal him. 'Come to me, all you who labour and are overburdened, and I will give you rest. Shoulder my yoke and learn from me, for I am gentle and humble in heart, and you will find rest for your souls! Yes, my yoke is easy and my burden light'.

James 1:2-4, 12

My brothers, you will always have your trials but, when they come, try to treat them as a happy privilege; you understand that your faith is only put to the test to make you patient, but patience too is to have its practical results so that you will become fully-developed, complete, with nothing missing. Happy the man who stands firm when trials come. He has proved himself, and will win the prize of life, the crown that the Lord has promised to those who love him.

Psalm 16:1-2, 5, 7-11

Look after me, God, I take shelter in you. To the LORD you say, 'My Lord, you are my fortune, nothing else but you'. LORD, my heritage, my cup, you, and you only, hold my lot secure; I bless the LORD, who is my counsellor, and in the night my inmost self instructs me; I keep the LORD before me always, for with him at my right hand nothing can shake me.

So my heart exults, my very soul rejoices, my body, too, will rest securely, for you will not abandon my soul to Sheol, nor allow the one you love to see the Pit; you will reveal the path of life to me, give me unbounded joy in your presence, and at your right hand everlasting pleasures.

Psalm 90:1-6, 10, 12

Lord, you have been our refuge age after age.

Before the mountains were born, before the earth or the world come to birth, you were God from all eternity and for ever.

You can turn man back into dust by saying, 'Back to what you were, you sons of men!'

To you, a thousand years are a single day, a yesterday now over, an hour of the night.

You brush men away like waking dreams, they are like grass sprouting and flowering in the morning, withered and dry before dusk.

Our life lasts for seventy years, eighty with good health, but they all add up to anxiety and trouble - over in a trice, and then we are gone.

Teach us to count how few days we have and so gain wisdom of heart.

Psalm 116:1-13

Alleluia! I love! For the LORD listens to my entreaty; he bends down to listen to me when I call.

Death's cords were tightening round me, the nooses of Sheol; distress and anguish gripped me, I invoked the name of the LORD.

'LORD, rescue me!' The LORD is righteous and merciful, our God is tenderhearted;

The LORD defends the simple, he saved me when I was brought to my knees.

Return to your resting place, my soul, the LORD has treated you kindly.

He has rescued me from death, my eyes from tears and my feet from stumbling.

I will walk in the LORD'S presence in the land of the living.

I have faith, even when I say, 'I am completely crushed'.

In my alarm, I declared, 'No man can be relied on'.

What return can I make to the LORD for all his goodness to me?

I will offer libations to my Saviour, invoking the name of the LORD.

Saints for the Sick

"...suffering belongs to the ups and downs of men and women throughout history, who must learn to accept and go beyond it. And yet how can they, if not thanks to the Cross of Christ?" – Pope John Paul II [7]

There is real help which transforms the sufferings of 'the sick' - be you only temporarily in hospital, or permanently crippled, diseased, chair-bound, in constant or intermittent pain. Those who have experienced this help are themselves the living evidence of its reality.

St Thérèse of Lisieux well summarised the reality of this involvement when she said, just before she died: 'I feel that my mission is soon to begin... I will spend my heaven doing good on earth. This is not impossible, since the angels from the very heart of the beatific vision keep watch over us. No, I shall not be able to take any rest until the end of the world'.

So, the saints are concerned with us, really hungering to help us win through. But they cannot force their help on us; they can enter only where they are invited. We must, in prayer, approach them.

No one knows or knew this better than the saints themselves. St Cyprian, for instance, was telling everybody: 'We should look to Heaven as our real home; there a great multitude awaits us of those who are freed from care for their own salvation but are full of care for ours'.

St Stanislaus teaches us 'in every trial in life, and above all in sickness and in the hour of death, to ask the prayer of our saint and to trust fearlessly in his aid'.

'Choose some particular saints', instructs St Francis de Sales, 'that you may enter more deeply into their spirit and imitate them, and have a special confidence in their intercession'. Here are a few of the saints waiting, now, for our approach.

St Camillus de Lellis

He suffered an obstinate disease in his leg which caused a painful deterioration of health for thirty years, terminating with his death in 1614, but his youth and early manhood were as 'worldly' as can be, with no interest in our Lord beyond the routines of a nominal Catholic.

His family were of the Italian nobility, and in his youth Camillus lived the self-indulgent life of the aristocracy of the time. He left home when he was seventeen to join an army, and he took part in killing and maiming with neither care nor mercy until he was ignominiously discharged after four years.

He was very big physically, very strong and constantly in trouble because of a violent temper, which combined with debts incurred by his passion for heavy gambling to place him in disgrace - even by army standards!

Beneath his dislikeable character he had a fine brain and profound mind and, like many before him and since, he came to realise the limitations and futility of values confined to life on earth. Inevitably, his gropings for the reason and purpose of life led him to God, and once he had made his choice God led him to a confessor.

He spent a long time in hospital, and it was largely in his sick-bed that his spiritual progress was made. He became gentler, developed patience, and learned to make his suffering a means of uniting himself with Christ. He worked hard at seeing the good in all men, which led to him seeking and finding Christ in the patients around him. And as his love for them grew, so did his concern for their welfare.

When he was well enough to leave the hospital, although his suffering from the disease continued, he studied for the priesthood and after initial trials and setbacks, the first congregation of the Servants of the Sick was confirmed by Pope Pius V in 1586.

Let us pray. *St Camillus, even as you spent your life in service to the poor and the sick, your heart and mind were firmly centred in the words of Jesus: "Blessed are the merciful for mercy will be theirs." You saw in the many poor and sick you cared for the truth that God never abandons his people even in their most difficult trials. Your hope in God's love was boundless. In our own lives, we often find ourselves having nothing and no one to count on. Often we are like the poor and the sick you cared for. Through your intercession, we pray that hope in God's love and mercy will be always in our hearts. In fact, even now, we hope for God's forgiveness of our sins, for His endless care and for this grace. This we ask through Christ, our Lord. Amen.*

St Paul of the Cross

He was racked with bodily pain through the last fifty of his eighty-one years of life, and he so completely associated his sufferings with Christ's that his joy in Christ quickly grew to outshine his suffering.

As a child of devout middle-class parents in their home in northern Italy, he had been taught by his mother that by accepting our suffering we are, in effect, relieving Christ of this suffering.

His offering of his pain to God began when he was over thirty years old. The pains that were to gnaw at him for fifty years first began when he was serving as a soldier in 1714.

He came back from crusading against the Turks and left the army in 1720 in compliance with a growing compulsion to bring people to Christ.

As a layman, even before he was ordained priest, he began to preach the Passion, and through his love of the crucified Jesus he felt the Holy Spirit leading him to found a congregation devoted to our Lord's suffering. The Order is today known as the Passionists.

Let us pray. *Paul, our father and brother, as we stand with you before the Cross of Christ may our minds, our hearts and our lives be overwhelmed by the love shown there for us. As you followed the example of Jesus Crucified may we too be emptied of all things but the desire to do God's will and so keep alive the memory of the Passion and Death of Jesus Christ our only hope. Amen.*

St Germaine

Meeting Christ in Holy Communion was the only friend St Germaine found throughout her life of suffering. She knew it all: the pain of prolonged illness, neglect and the thoughtlessness of others.

Germaine was born at Pibrac in France in 1579, the only daughter of a farm labourer by the name of Cousin. While she was still an infant, her mother died and the child soon had a stepmother who was despicably cruel to her, never allowing her to play with her stepbrothers or sisters, forever chastising her, hitting her, and making work hard in the house. She would fetch and carry food for the family but was never allowed to eat with them, she herself only receiving what was left over. Life was difficult for her and on top of this she was also subjected to the cruelty of the villagers, who ridiculed her for her deformity and constant illnesses.

By the time she was in her early teens, the attitude of the villagers began to change. The unhappiness and cruelty of her home and the pain and suffering she endured were relentless, but despite this she would always be ready to do all she could for other in the village. Her reputation for being gentle and compassionate began to spread.

Germaine's 'garland of joy' was the children who, in time, gathered round her to listen as she told them of Christ and his mother and his saints, and her gentle goodness was something the children never forgot.

Let us pray. *O Saint Germaine, look down from Heaven and intercede for the many sick children in our world. Help them to sanctify these sufferings. Strengthen children who suffer from disease or sickness. Protect those children who have been abandoned by their parents and live in the streets. Intercede for children with disabilities and their parents. Saint Germaine, you who suffered neglect so patiently, pray for us. Amen.*

St Peregrine

Peregrine Laziosi was a 13th century Servite brother, who is known today as the patron saint of people with cancer or malignancy of any kind.

Peregrine was about thirty years old when he entered the Servites as a lay brother. His days were spent in prayer, work in the monastery and visiting the poor and sick in the town.

Peregrine offered no magic cures or promises of recovery. He simply brought compassion to the dying, and comfort and support for the bereaved. His presence among them as a Servite brother was witness to his faith in a God who continued to care for and love all people regardless of their state of health.

Peregrine developed varicose veins and his condition progressively worsened until one of his legs eventually became ulcerated and malignant. Dr Paul de Salaghis, the local medical practitioner, was called in. After examination, the doctor recommended amputation as the only hope of saving Brother Peregrine's life.

That night, Peregrine lay in bed considering his predicament. Operations in those times, six hundred years before the arrival of anaesthesia as we know it today, could be grim affairs. Surgical instruments were often crude. Disinfectants were unknown, which meant that many patients died from infection following amputation or other surgery.

So the odds against Peregrine's survival were high, operation or no operation. In the middle of the night and in great pain, he dragged himself out of bed to pray before a crucifix in the monastery chapter room.

An old history of the saint written in the 15th century records how Peregrine fell asleep in front of the crucifix, and in a dream seemed to see Jesus come down from the cross. He woke up and made his way back to bed.

In the morning the doctor arrived with his instruments to perform the amputation. On examination of the leg he found that the wound had healed and there was no sign of gangrene. The operation was cancelled and the doctor departed in amazement. Word of the dramatic recovery spread like wildfire throughout the town. The Servite brother was restored to health and continued his work among the sick.

Let us pray. *Glorious wonder-worker, St Peregrine, you answered the divine call with a ready spirit, and forsook all the comforts of a life of ease and all the empty honours of the world to dedicate yourself to God in the Order of His holy Mother.*

You laboured manfully for the salvation of souls. In union with Jesus crucified, you endured painful sufferings with such patience as to deserve to be healed miraculously of an incurable cancer in your leg by a touch of His divine hand.

Obtain for me the grace to answer every call of God and to fulfill His will in all the events of life. Enkindle in my heart a consuming zeal for the salvation of all men. Deliver me from the infirmities that afflict my body (especially...).

Obtain for me also a perfect resignation to the sufferings it may please God to send me, so that, imitating our crucified Saviour and His sorrowful Mother, I may merit eternal glory in heaven.

St Bernadette

In 1858, Bernadette, a little girl intellectually backward and physically ill, left her home one day in Lourdes to gather sticks by the side of the River Gave, because they were too poor at home to afford coal for their fire. In reality, her home was little more than a hovel; they lived in an old disused prison. As she and her brother and sister came along the riverbank, they reached a canal. Bernadette, fearing the cold water, was afraid to cross. Her brother and sister laughed at her and left her behind.

Bernadette stooped down to remove her stockings, when suddenly she heard the sound of wind in the trees, and looking up she saw Our Lady in a grotto and surrounded by a golden light. Bernadette fell on her knees. Our Lady appeared thus to Bernadette several times and often spoke to her. She told her that she wished people to come here in procession and to do penance for their souls and the souls of others. She told her to make a hole in the sand, and water flowed forth.

Many years have passed, and this grotto, then unknown, is one of the best known and most loved places in the world. Miracles of healing have taken place through the spring of water which was unsealed at the touch of Bernadette's hand.

While Lourdes was passing from glory to glory, where was Bernadette? Hidden in her convent at Nevers: stricken with sickness. What was she doing? One day some visitors asked her if she had heard of some of the recent wonders of Lourdes. She answered no. The visitors could not understand how this could be. Bernadette replied, 'You see, my business is to be ill'.

It was her business to be ill because it was the business given her direct from heaven. She suffered very greatly and in 1879 died a painful death. That suffering and death made her a saint and was her path straight to heaven, because she accepted it as her business, sent to her direct from her heavenly Father. And therefore it was her greatest treasure.

Let us pray. *O God, protector and lover of the humble, You bestowed on Your servant, Bernadette, the favour of the vision of Our Lady, the Immaculate Virgin Mary, and of speech with her. Grant that we may deserve to behold You in heaven. Amen. St Bernadette pray for us.*

Sacrament of Penance

"The kind of God we adore is one who looks out always for us, wanting us to return constantly to him, and when he sees us, takes pity on us, throws his arms around our neck and kisses us." - Cardinal Basil Hume OSB

Examination of conscience

Sorrow for our sins and a desire to change direction and not to sin again are at the centre of our reconciliation with our Lord and his Church. Before approaching the sacrament we need to prepare ourselves by prayer and examining our conscience.

Preparation

Almighty and merciful God, you have brought me here in the name of your Son to receive your mercy and grace in my time of need. Open my eyes to see what I have done. Touch my heart and convert me to yourself. Where sin has separated me from you, may your love unite me to you again: where sin has brought weakness, may your power heal and strengthen; where sin has bought death, may your Spirit raise to new life. Give me a new heart to love you, so that my life may reflect the image of your Son. Amen.

Reading from Scripture

One of the most marvellous gifts we have is the Word of God set down in Holy Scripture. Through the Word we receive light to recognise our sins; through it we will understand the change of heart and mind to which our Lord invites us; through it we will grow in confidence in God's mercy.

'See, today I set before you life and prosperity, death and disaster. If you obey the commandments of the Lord your God, if you love the Lord your God and follow his ways, you will live and increase and the Lord your God will bless you. Choose life, then, so that you may live in the love of the Lord your God.' (*Deuteronomy* 30:15-16, 19)

'I will give them a single heart and I will put a new spirit in them; I will remove the heart of stone from their bodies and give them a heart of flesh instead, so that they will keep my laws and respect my observances and put them into practice. Then they shall be my people and I will be their God.' (*Ezekiel* 11:19-20)

How do I begin?

I am here to be reconciled to God and to my neighbour. So I must confess my sins, the sins that burden my conscience, to receive once again the gift of God's forgiveness.

Examining my conscience

Let us consider the first great commandment of our Lord.

'You shall love the Lord your God with all your heart, and with all your soul, and with all your mind, and with all you strength'.

- When making important decisions about my way of life, have I put God first?
- Am I so caught up with getting on in this world that I give no thought to the things of God?
- Have I set aside the Church's teaching and gone my own way?
- Have I really trusted God, especially in times of difficulty?
- Have I prayed in times of temptation?
- Is my heart set on money, on my own amusement at any cost?

'You shall love your neighbour as yourself'.

- Do I use other people for my own ends and advantage?
- In my family life, do I really try to fulfil my responsibilities, as father or mother, husband or wife, son or daughter? Do I make my home a happy and loving place by being tolerant and forgiving, giving the others consideration and supporting them in their personal difficulties?

- Do I show proper respect for the other members of my family, recognising that disobedience can be a sin when I deliberately defy my parents?
- As a parent, have I done my best to provide for both the spiritual and material needs of my children?
- Have I been faithful to my husband (wife)?
- Do I spend the proper amount of my wages or any other money I have on the family, or do I spend it on other things?
- Do I despise others, particularly those of other races or religions?
- In my work am I just, hard-working, honest? Do I cheat or break agreements or contracts?
- Have I been truthful and fair? Have I deliberately deceived others? Judged them rashly? Injured their reputation by lies about them? Have I been cruel?
- Do I hate people - and keep up a long-standing hatred?
- Have I stolen the property of others or planned to get hold of what belongs to another?
- Have I forgiven an injury? Have I sought revenge?
- Do I accept responsibility for my own life and destiny?
- Am I envious, proud and arrogant? Am I domineering?
- How do I use my gifts and talents?
- Do I complain about misfortunes? Or do I accept suffering and disappointment?

- Have I been chaste and pure? Or have I toyed with temptations to impurity - by deliberately looking for what is impure?
- Have I dishonoured my body for fornication, impurity, foul conversation, lusting thoughts, unchaste actions?
- Have I given in to sensuality, particularly in my reading or my entertainments?

Prayer of sorrow

The most important things you do in the celebration of the Sacrament of Penance are to recognise and to be sorry for what you have done wrong and then relying on God's help and love for you to make up your mind to live differently. This is not necessarily a matter of feeling tearful about your sins, nor yet again does it mean that you have to try to shut out of your mind the possibility that you will in fact fall again. It is much more a matter of really and genuinely making up your mind to try to live your whole life in the light of the holiness and love of God.

THE SACRAMENT OF PENANCE

Pr. In the name of the Father, and of the Son, and of the Holy Spirit. Amen.

The invitation to trust

The Priest will briefly invite you to have confidence and trust in God. This is the point in confession for you to tell the Priest about yourself, if you are someone he does not already know. You should tell him anything which may help him to help you in your spiritual life; for instance, when you last went to confession, whether you are married or not, and the main difficulties which you have in trying to live the Christian life.

The Word of God

Next the Priest, or you yourself at his invitation, may choose to read an appropriate passage of Holy Scripture proclaiming God's mercy and calling men to conversion.

1 Peter 1:18-21 - Remember the ransom that was paid to free you was not paid in anything corruptible, neither in silver nor gold, but in the precious blood of a lamb without stain, namely Christ. Through him you now have faith in God, who raised him from the dead and gave him glory for that very reason - so that you would have faith and hope in God.

1 John 1:8-9; 2:1-2 - If we say we have no sin in us, we are deceiving ourselves and refusing to admit the truth; but if we acknowledge our sins, then God who is faithful and just will forgive our sins and purify us from everything that is wrong. We have our advocate with the Father, Jesus Christ, who is just; he is the sacrifice that takes our sins away, and not only ours, but the whole world's.

Confession, counsel and reconciliation

Where it is the custom, you now say a general formula for confession (for example: I confess to almighty God). You then confess your sins. You may speak in a normal conversational manner. Listen to any advice the Priest may give you, and ask him questions if you do not understand anything.

The Priest proposes a penance which you accept to make satisfaction for sin and to amend your life. This penance will serve not only to make up for the past but also to help you begin a new life and provide you with the antidote to weakness. As far as possible, the penance will correspond to the seriousness and nature of the sins. It may suitably take the form of prayer, self-denial, and especially service of your neighbour and works of mercy. These will underline the fact that sin and its forgiveness have a social aspect.

The Priest will then ask you to express your sorrow:

Act of Contrition

Pen. My God, I am sorry for my sins with all my heart. In choosing to do wrong and failing to do good, I have sinned against you whom I should love above all things. I firmly intend, with your help, to do penance, to sin no more, and to avoid whatever leads me to sin. Our Saviour Jesus Christ suffered and died for us. In his name, my God, have mercy. Amen.

Absolution

If you are not kneeling, bow your head as the Priest extends his hands (or at least extends his right hand), and pronounces the words of absolution, as follows:
Pr. God, the Father of mercies, through the death and resurrection of his Son has reconciled the world to himself and sent the Holy Spirit among us for the forgiveness of sins; through the ministry of the Church may God give you pardon and peace, and I absolve you from your sins in the name of the Father, and of the Son, and of the Holy Spirit. Amen.

Conclusion of the Rite

After the absolution the Priest may continue:
Pr. Give thanks to the Lord, for he is good.
You reply: Pen. His mercy endures forever.
Then the Priest dismisses you saying:
Pr. The Lord has freed you from your sins. Go in peace.

Thanksgiving

*At the conclusion of the rite you leave the place of
confession. No matter what the penance given you was,
you now have the opportunity to reflect on what has taken
place and to thank God for his mercy and forgiveness:*

Almighty and merciful God, how wonderfully you
created man and still more wonderfully remade him. You
do not abandon the sinner but seek him out with a father's
love. You sent your Son into the world to destroy sin and
death by his passion, and to restore life and joy by his
resurrection. You sent the Holy Spirit into my heart
making me one of your children and an heir of your
kingdom. You constantly renew my spirit in the
sacraments of your redeeming love, freeing me from
slavery to sin and transforming me ever more closely into
the likeness of your beloved Son. Thank you for the
wonders of your mercy. Glory to you through Christ, in
the Holy Spirit, now and forever. Amen.

Communion when Sick

"...the vocation of every Christian is truly that of being together with Jesus, bread that is broken for the life of the World." - Pope Benedict XVI[8]

When the Priest or commissioned minister of Holy Communion enter, they will greet you.

P. The Lord be with you.
R. And with your spirit.

The Penitential Rite

The minister will then invite you to call your sins to mind, and after a short pause, will lead you in one of the forms of the Penetential Act.

1. P. You were sent to heal the contrite of heart:
Lord, have mercy.
R. Lord, have mercy.
P. You came to call sinners: Christ, have mercy.
R. Christ, have mercy.
P. You are seated at the right hand of the Father to intercede for us: Lord, have mercy.
R. Lord, have mercy.

2. I confess to almighty God and to you, my brothers and sisters, that I have greatly sinned, in my thoughts and in my words, in what I have done and in what I have failed to do, (And, striking their breast, they say:) through my fault, through my fault, through my most grievous fault; therefore I ask blessed Mary ever-Virgin, all the Angels and Saints, and you, my brothers and sisters, to pray for me to the Lord our God.

At the end of the rite of penance, the minister says the absolution.

P. May almighty God have mercy on us, forgive us our sins, and bring us to everlasting life.

R. Amen.

Liturgy of the Word

The minister may now read from scripture then give a brief explanation of the reading, applying it to the needs of the sick person and those who are looking after him or her. General intercessions may also be said.

Communion Rite

The minister goes on to invite all present to join in saying:

P. At the Saviour's command and formed by divine teaching, we dare to say:

R. Our Father, who art in heaven, hallowed be thy name; thy kingdom come; thy will be done on earth as it is in heaven. Give us this day our daily bread; and forgive us our trespasses as we forgive those who trespass against us; and lead us not into temptation but deliver us from evil. Amen.

The minister then shows the Holy Eucharist to those present and says:

P. Behold the Lamb of God, behold him who takes away the sins of the world. Blessed are those called to the supper of the Lamb.

R. Lord, I am not worthy that you should enter under my roof, but only say the word and my soul shall be healed.

The minister then says: The body of Christ. R. Amen.

You then receive Holy Communion, as do any of the others present who wish to. Afterwards the minister offers a short concluding prayer.

R. Amen.

The minister will then bless you. R. Amen.

Prayer after Holy Communion

O Jesus, I believe that I have received your Flesh to eat and your Blood to drink, because you have said it, and your word is true. All that I have and all that I am are your gift and now you have given me yourself.

O Jesus, my God, my Creator, I adore you, because from your hands I came and with you I am to be happy forever.

O Jesus, I am not worthy to receive you, and yet you have come to me that my poor heart may learn of you to be meek and humble.

Jesus, I love you; I love you with all my heart. You know that I love you, and wish to love you daily more and more.

My good Jesus, I thank you with all my heart. How good, how kind you are to me. Blessed be Jesus in the most holy Sacrament of the Altar.

Anointing of the Sick

"When we walk with the Lord, we leave with him our burdens, and this confers the strength to accomplish the mission he gives us. He who takes from us gives to us; he takes upon himself our weakness and gives us his strength."
– Pope John Paul II [9]

TEACHING OF THE CHURCH

Often the gravest problems we have to face in life are illness and suffering. Illness, particularly, makes us experience our powerlessness, our limits, our finiteness; it even gives us a glimpse of death. Being ill can lead some to rebel against God, to become anxious, alone and despairing. Yet, very often sickness can help us search and return to God and can help us to discern about what really is important. Certainly, an illness can make a person more mature.

Where is God in all this, I ask myself? - As surely have many others. The Scriptures speak of this. In the Old Testament, there are people who lived their sickness in the presence of God, imploring help and healing from God the giver of life and death. Sickness was often the start of a journey of a change of heart - a time of conversion.

One great hope shines out from the life of Christ - his great compassion for the sick and the weak. He has the power to heal and much more - to forgive our sins. He is the physician who has come to heal us profoundly and completely - body and soul. This compassion moved Christ to make the miseries of the suffering sick who touched him his own. It is still true that he did not heal all the sick - his healing indicated a more radical healing he had prepared for all of us - the healing made possible through his great victory over death, and sin, by passing through death itself in his own Passover. So, by his own passion, death and resurrection Christ gives new meaning to suffering - it unites us to him.

Christ has extended to each of us an invitation, which until today, may have meant little. Take up your cross and follow me, as a disciple. By following Christ with our own cross, we his disciples acquire a new outlook on illness, and on the sick. It is true that even the most intense prayers do not always obtain the healing of a sickness: as St Paul learnt from the Lord - 'my grace is sufficient for you, for my power is made perfect in weakness'. He learnt that by suffering we can complete in our own flesh what is lacking in Christ's afflictions for the sake of his Body, the Church.

The Sacrament of the Sick

Among the Church's seven sacraments, the Anointing of the Sick is especially meant to strengthen those who are being tried by illness. It was instituted by Christ and anointing the sick with blessed oil has long been the Church's practice, while begging for recovery or preparing for death itself.

This Sacrament is given to the seriously ill by anointing them on the forehead and hands with blessed oil. It is given as soon as someone, through old age or sickness, begins to be in danger of death; it is not just meant for those at the point of death. It is as good for the elderly and frail, as for someone preparing for a serious operation. It can be given more than once, and only by a Priest, and always the Christian community is involved through it to surround and support their sick brother, in prayer and affection.

Jesus instructed his Church to heal the sick, and this she does by caring and praying for them, and bringing his life-giving presence through the sacraments of Penance, the Eucharist and of the Sick. Leaving his apostles to continue his work, he directed them to 'go out to the whole world, proclaim the Good News to all creation', adding this: 'These are the signs that will be associated with believers... they will lay their hands on the sick, who will recover.' He left it to one of his apostles, St James, to announce the gift of a special healing and comforting Sacrament: 'Is any one among you suffering? Let him pray. Is any one among you sick? Let him call for the elders of the Church, and let them pray over him, anointing him with oil in the name of the Lord; and the prayer of faith will save the sick man, and the Lord will raise him up; and if he has committed sins, he will be forgiven'. (*James* 5:13-15)

How is the Sacrament celebrated?

It is very simple, and can take place at home, in hospital or in Church. Normally it starts with an act of repentance, followed by listening to a reading from the Gospel, a moment for reflection and explanation. Then after prayers, calling on the Holy Spirit to strengthen the sick, the Priest lays his hands on the sick person. Then the forehead and hands are anointed. After further prayers, there can be Holy Communion.

It is very fitting to precede this with the Sacrament of Penance; and then to celebrate it inside the Eucharist itself.

This Sacrament confers special graces on the sick: firstly strength, peace and courage to overcome the difficulties of serious illness or old age. The Holy Spirit strengthens against the temptation to discouragement and anguish, and leads the sick person to a healing of the soul - or even the body if it is God's will - and forgiveness of sins. Secondly, the sick person is given the gift of closer unity to Christ's passion, and participates in Jesus' saving work and contributes to the sanctification of the Church through their own suffering. Lastly, it completes in a very real way the holy anointings that mark the whole Christian life, Baptism and Confirmation. It fortifies us for the final struggle prior to entering our Father's House.

THE RITE OF ANOINTING OF THE SICK

Introductory Rites

Greeting
The Priest approaches the sick person and greets him and the others present in a friendly manner.
P. The peace of the Lord be with you always.
R. And with your spirit.

Instruction
Then the Priest addresses those present in these or similar words:
Lord God you have said to us through your apostle James: 'Are there people sick among you? Let them send for the priests of the Church, and let the priests pray over them anointing them with oil in the name of the Lord. The prayer of faith will save the sick persons, and the Lord will raise them up. If they have committed any sins their sins will be forgiven them.' Lord we are gathered

here in your name and we ask you to be among us, to watch over our brother/sister N. We ask this with confidence, for you live and reign for ever and ever.
R. Amen.

Liturgy of Anointing

Laying on of hands
In silence the Priest lays his hands on the head of the sick person.

Anointing
The Priest takes the oil and anoints the sick person. He anoints first on the forehead, saying:
P. Through this holy anointing may the Lord in his love and mercy help you with the grace of the Holy Spirit.
R. Amen.
Then on the hands, saying:
P. May the Lord who frees you from sin save you and raise you up. R. Amen.

The Lord's Prayer
The Priest introduces the Lord's Prayer in these or similar words:
P. Now let us pray to God as our Lord Jesus Christ taught us:
All say: Our Father…

Prayer after Anointing
The Priest may say:
P. Father in heaven, through this holy anointing grant N. comfort in his/her suffering.

When he/she is afraid, give him/her courage, when afflicted, give him/her patience, when dejected, afford him/her hope, and when alone, assure him/her of the support of your holy people. We ask this through Christ our Lord. R. Amen.

Concluding Rite

Blessing
The Priest will conclude by blessing the patient saying:
P. May the blessing of almighty God, the Father, and the Son, and the Holy Spirit, come upon you and remain with you for ever. R. Amen.

Night Prayer

V. O God, come to our aid.
R. O Lord, make haste to help us.
    Glory be to the Father...
Here an examination of conscience is commended.

Hymn
Now it is evening; time to cease from labour,
Father, according to thy will and pleasure,
Through the night-season, have thy faithful people
Safe in thy keeping.

Far from our dwellings drive the evil spirits;
Under the shadow of thy wings protect us;
Be thou our guardian through the hours of darkness,
Strong to defend us.

Call we, ere sleeping, on the name of Jesus;
Rise we at day-break, strong to serve thee better;
Order our goings, well begun and ended,
All to thy glory.

Fountain of goodness, bless the sick and needy;
Visit the captive, solace the afflicted;
Shelter the stranger, feed your starving children;
Strengthen the dying.

Father, who neither slumberest nor sleepest,
Thou, to whom darkness is as clear as noonday,
Have us this night-time, for the sake of Jesus,
Safe in thy keeping.[10]

Psalmody
Ant. He will conceal you with his wings; you will not
fear the terror of the night.

In the shelter of the Most High   Psalm 90 (91)
Behold, I have given you power to tread underfoot
serpents and scorpions (Lk 10:19)

He who dwells in the shelter of the Most High *
and abides in the shade of the Almighty
says to the Lord: 'My refuge, *
my stronghold, my God in whom I trust!'

It is he who will free you from the snare *
of the fowler who seeks to destroy you;
he will conceal you with his pinions *
and under his wings you will find refuge.

You will not fear the terror of the night *
nor the arrow that flies by day,
nor the plague that prowls in the darkness *
nor the scourge that lays waste at noon.

A thousand may fall at your side, *
ten thousand fall at your right,
you, it will never approach; *
his faithfulness is buckler and shield.

Your eyes have only to look *
to see how the wicked are repaid,
you who have said: 'Lord, my refuge!' *
and have made the Most High your dwelling.

Upon you no evil shall fall,*
no plague approach where you dwell.
For you has he commanded his angels, *
to keep you in all your ways.

They shall bear you upon their hands *
lest you strike your foot against a stone.
On the lion and the viper you will tread *
and trample the young lion and the dragon.

Since he clings to me in love, I will free him; *
protect him for he knows my name.
When he calls I shall answer: I am with you.' *
I will save him in distress and give him glory.

With length of life I will content him; *
I shall let him see my saving power.   (Glory be...)

Ant. He will conceal you with his wings; you will not fear the terror of the night.

Scripture Reading (*Rv* 22:4-5)

They will see the Lord face to face, and his name will be written on their foreheads. It will never be night again and they will not need lamplight or sunlight, because the Lord God will be shining on them. They will reign for ever and ever.

Short Responsory

R. Into your hands, Lord, I commend my spirit. (Repeat)

V. You have redeemed us, Lord God of truth.

R. Into your hands, Lord, I commend my spirit.

Glory be to the Father...

R. Into your hands, Lord, I commend my spirit.

Ant. Save us, Lord, while we are awake; protect us while we sleep; that we may keep watch with Christ and rest with him in peace.

Nunc dimittis (*Canticle: Lk 2:29-32*)

Christ is the light of the nations and the glory of Israel

At last, all-powerful Master, †

you give leave to your servant *

to go in peace, according to your promise.

For my eyes have seen your salvation *
Which you have prepared for all nations,
the light to enlighten the Gentiles *
and give glory to Israel, your people.   (Glory be...)

Ant. Save us, Lord, while we are awake; protect us while
we sleep; that we may keep watch with Christ and rest
with him in peace.

Concluding Prayer
God our Father, as we have celebrated today the mystery
of the Lord's resurrection, grant our humble prayer: free
us from all harm that we may sleep in peace and rise in
joy to sing your praise. Through Christ our Lord.

Blessing
The Lord grant us a quiet night and a perfect end.
R. Amen.

Anthem to the Blessed Virgin Mary
Hail, holy Queen, mother of mercy; hail, our life, our
sweetness, and our hope! To you do we cry, poor banished
children of Eve; to you do we send up our sighs, mourning
and weeping in this vale of tears. Turn then, most gracious
advocate, your eyes of mercy towards us; and after this
our exile, show to us the blessed fruit of your womb,
Jesus. O clement, O loving, O sweet Virgin Mary.

Endnotes

¹ *3ʳᵈ World Day of Prayer for the Sick.*

² *5ᵗʰ World Day of Prayer of the Sick.*

³ *9th World Day of Prayer of the Sick.*

⁴ *'To be a Pilgrim'.*

⁵ *4ᵗʰ World Day of Prayer of the Sick.*

⁶ *7ᵗʰ World Day of Prayer of the Sick.*

⁷ *12ᵗʰ World Day of Prayer of the Sick.*

⁸ *16ᵗʰ World Day of Prayer of the Sick.*

⁹ *'Ecclesia in Oceania' (2001)*

¹⁰ P. Herbert d. 1571, Tr G. R. Woodward 1848-1934
and compilers of The BBC Hymn Book.

LIGHTHOUSE TALKS™

CAN YOU TRUST GOD?
DR. TIM GRAY

Dr. Gray addresses the pervasive misconceptions that God is quick to anger, that the God of the Old and New Testaments are different, and that God doesn't have a merciful heart for us.

MEN AND WOMEN ARE FROM EDEN
DR. MARY HEALY

With incredible clarity, Dr. Healy explains how the *Theology of the Body* is astonishingly good news for a culture littered with broken marriages, immorality, heartache, and loneliness.

DISCOVER WHY LIGHTHOUSE TALKS HAVE REACHED
MORE THAN 15 MILLION LISTENERS ACROSS THE GLOBE

To learn more, visit us at
augustineinstitute.org/audio
or call (866) 767-3155